The Path of a Goddess™

Womb Healing Workbook

Overcoming Childhood Sexual Abuse

Prompts, Prayer, and Ritual

Updated First Edition

By Tahtahme

Intended for Ages 18+

Note: This is the same workbook as "Sexual Abuse", but modified for sexual abuse endured during childhood.

*This workbook is to be used as a tool
to aid you on your journey to overcome
childhood sexual abuse
and heal your womb.*

Table of Contents

Dear Goddess,

Looking back on the journey I have had, from the small child with no one she could trust, all the way to the powerful woman who embraces her divine femininity, I cannot help but be reminded of the lotus.

Beginning in the mud and murky depths, the lotus grows down first, rooting itself and pushing upwards, eventually emerging in all perfection above it all, displayed gloriously and emanating the true essence of success and beauty.

Let us be like the lotus, sis, let us reach down into the mud of our past, steady our foundation with a strong and critical eye, and then rise, ready to blossom into our future. Let us be not afraid of the dirt of yesterday, or of the glory that is to come.

May we rise, and may we bloom.

Peace on your path,

Tahtahme Nehendas Xero

Bastet Priestess

Sacred Woman

Womb Worker

thepathofagoddess@gmail.com

[Part One]

The Goal

Let's begin by deciding what you want from this journey. Seriously. Spell it out. There is power in words, let's go ahead speak that future into existence. What exactly do you hope to gain from taking this journey?

Peace of mind? Acceptance? Happiness? Family? Let's make a plan. It helps to see it laid out.

When you answer these questions, answer naturally--you do not have to make connections always to your sexual abuse. In many ways we are envisioning a life where we do not think of the abuse as often, as painfully, or carry it's weight as heavily on our shoulders.

To me, overcoming my sexual abuse means:

The part of my journey I am most excited about is:

The part of my journey I am most scared of is:

Who would benefit from me taking this healing journey?

Who would benefit from me *not* taking this healing journey?

What skills do I believe I will have once I overcome my sexual abuse?

What skills do I believe I will never have because I was sexually abused?

What do I think will happen when I overcome my sexual abuse?

Who do I think will be happiest about me overcoming my sexual abuse?
Why?

When I imagine my future, I see:

I am healing myself for:

I am worth healing because:

By this time next year, I see myself…

Five years from now, I will be....

When I am 90 years old, I see myself…

[Part Two]

The Path To Self Love

Okay enough procrastinating, you have put this off for long enough. It is time to accept yourself. As you are. Today. Right now. We aren't messing around, sis, we are jumping right in.

I want you to be unapologetically entranced with your inner *and* outer self. I want you to smile when you look in the mirror, I want you to know at all times that you are ready and lovely and worth it. I want you to know you are everything.

This section can be worked through page by page or you can do as many prompts from this section day by day as you like. But when you do the prompts, really savor and meditate on them. Really experience them. Do them again if it doesn't work the first time. Healing is a process and requires your patience. Don't give up.

List 100 Things You Love, Like, Or Enjoy About Yourself

These things can be big or small, significant or insignificant, as shallow or deep as you can think of. Just write them down as you think of the qualities you have. Start with what you can think of and come back to fill out more and reread the amazing things that make you you!

1)

2)

3)

4)

5)

6)

7)

8)

9)

10)

11)

12)

13)

14)

15)

16)

17)

18)

19)

20)

21)

22)

23)

24)

25)

26)

27)

28)

29)

30)

31)

32)

33)

34)

35)

36)

37)

38)

39)

40)

41)

42)

43)

44)

45)

46)

47)

48)

49)

50)

51)

52)

53)

54)

55)

56)

57)

58)

59)

60)

61)

62)

63)

64)

65)

66)

67)

68)

69)

70)

71)

72)

73)

74)

75)

76)

77)

78)

79)

80)

81)

82)

83)

84)

85)

86)

87)

88)

89)

90)

91)

92)

93)

94)

95)

96)

97)

98)

99)

100)

I was not playing, I want every space filled, too! When you finish, consider making a poster, or typing them up and hanging them somewhere you can see them when necessary, especially at times when you feel that you are unworthy, useless, or no good. You aren't any of those things...your list is testament to that. These are 100 reasons you are wonderful, necessary, and make the world a better place!

Did you have any thoughts or reflections from this challenge?

30 Day Body & Soul Self Love Challenge

For 30 days you will stand or sit in front of a large mirror and become acquainted with your naked body and vulnerable self. The beginning of each days challenge should always be Undressing With Purpose (detailed in Day One), and the end of each journaling session should be a five minute relaxed meditation, laying on your back or sitting cross legged to gently ease out of the session.

In these thirty days, find rituals and practices that stand out to you, and continue to incorporate them throughout your day to day life!

Tools Needed Throughout:

- ☐ A mirror large enough to see most of your body in.
- ☐ A private room
- ☐ 30 minutes to an hour daily
- ☐ Pens, markers and colored pencils for journaling and drawing
- ☐ A timer
- ☐ Beautiful scarf
- ☐ Notecards
- ☐ Candles

☐ Various common herbs

☐ Castor oil

Day One:

Undressing With Purpose

Stand in front of your mirror fully clothed. Study your face. Study your body.

What do you like the best about your body in this moment? (Feel free to write your thoughts each day as you go along, or in reflection, in the space provided below!)

Do your best to think only positive thoughts. Watch yourself as you undress. Do so gently and with deliberate movements, nothing unnecessary, remaining smooth. Appreciate the movements that your body makes, your body your own muse, luscious in its very existence.

Undressing With Purpose does *not* always have to be done in front of the mirror. You can take time and purpose without. But for this 30 Day Challenge, we will do this everyday before completing each day's exercise.

As much as possible, each day's challenge should be performed privately, nude, and in front of a large mirror.

Write your immediate reflection on this exercise:

Day Two:

Your Inner Goddess

I keep using this word "goddess", and I have yet to define it! In my heart the Goddess is the distinctly feminine archetype within, the grand power that rests in your soul on which all legends are based. When we embark on "The Path of the Goddess" we accept all the facets within us that make us whole we recognize the utter strength of the divine feminine, and we reclaim ourselves, our power, and our community.

Today we simply say a "how *you* been" to our inner Goddess. So leave your inhibitions in your clothes pile on the floor and let's get started.

Get close to the mirror. Look at each inch of your body. Pose. Each time pause for 5 to 10 seconds to really love what you see. Even if you can't, try. Try to see the Goddess inside, and compliment yourself on at least one thing *physically* every time.

Did you know models do this? They know every angle of their body. They know what they look like. They are intimate with themselves. Do the same courtesy to yourself and your vessel. Don't you deserve to know this part of you that others look at all day? Don't you get to enjoy it?

Try to do this every time you get in front of the mirror. Look at yourself a few different ways, enjoying yourself more each time. Flirt with yourself. Try never to leave the mirror until you have one beautiful moment, even if only for a second. Every time you complete the exercise, it becomes more effortless to spot the Goddess lurking behind your eyes.

What do you think it means to have a "goddess within"? Were you able to see your inner Goddess today?

Day Three:

Simply meditate on the glory of your body and mind. How wild is it that you are here? That you have all these thoughts, this intricate story of how you made it where you are today. Each tiny choice you made brought you here, each tiny (or big) thing to happen to you changed you little by little to get to this point...

And really that goes even further when you consider all of your hundreds of thousands of ancestors! All those people happening to meet, and love, and connect, and hate, and break up, and move, and procreate, and *take a chance,* all leading to...you. Here today. They all were here and the end result was you!

Beyond that, just who the heck and what the heck really are you? Who put you here? Are you worth that honor? Is anyone? Why or why not? Try to be as cohesive as you can with your thoughts on this as you reflect on this prompt.

Day Four:

Look at your naked body. Appreciate the curves as well as the flat planes.

Say, "My body is made beautifully."

Do you believe yourself when you say this? Maybe in some ways you do, but in others not so much? Why do you think this way? What exactly is wrong with any one body feature or type?

At times in the past it may have seemed that your body betrayed you. Like something was your bodies fault. Like maybe if you were a different weight, skin color, maybe if you had curves here and not there, or had a different personality, none of this would have happened.

Sis, I am here to tell you that if you think it, it is most likely true, but that burden is *not* on your body. It is not your body's fault. It does not make your body any less beautiful.

Has your body not been here through all this, and here it is, still pumping your heart, still sending creative energy through your womb center, working through the abuse not only others but you perhaps as well have inflicted on it? What more could you possibly ask? Your body has in so many, many ways been the most loyal body you have ever been around.

Say it again, "My body is made beautifully. It always has been."

What are habits you think you should change in how you speak about and to your body every day? If you feel you already speak and feed wellness to your body, there is always room to continue your growth in your journey with an ever changing body. This can also be a space to consider how you want your relationship with your body to be as you grow older.

Day Five:

Write 10 affirmations and place them on the walls and furniture in your living space.

Examples:

- Everything I seek now is seeking me.

- My womb is a well of abundance.
- I am the phoenix, the fiery sun, consuming and resuming myself. •
  Book of Coming Forth by Day
- Yes!
- Life is a beautiful and loving experience.
- I am beautifully made.
- I can!
- My womb is a well of strength.
- I can create anything I desire.
- I will!
- Fortune favors the bold.
- I have the heart of a lion.
- There is no one else who has what I have.
- I have so much to offer the world.

Brainstorm a few more:

Day Six:

Set a timer for 20 minutes, sit in front of the mirror, and stare into your own eyes. Look deep into them and try not to look away. What do you see? Who do you see?

Look at all the facets of yourself, the lover, the healer, the friend, the recluse, the diva, the queen, the hermit, the adventuress, the terrified, and the fearless.

See the utter love and abundance you have to offer. Relish in it. It is yours and only yours.

When the alarm rings, turn away from the mirror. Reflect:

Day Seven:

A wonderful exercise for confidence is to make faces in the mirror. Seriously. Practice common facial expressions such as smiling and laughing. Practice being serious and flirty. Give yourself a few good pouts and look your own anger in the eye. Even give a go at being silly or childish.

See which angles you feel your face and body look nicest in. Note your posture--try to straighten your spine and keep your shoulders back. Even try expressions you don't use very often, just to witness for yourself!

Knowing what you look like helps with confidence when you are in the moment.

Which expressions did you decide to practice? What are some habits you noticed today in the mirror that you hadn't realized you had?

Day Eight:

Femininity should be felt in every fiber of your being, in every body part. each toe should feel the electric energy of your inherent feminine nature. Turn on music with some drums and a beat...preferably from your own ancestry if you have even a vague idea of where your family is from.

The ancient art of dancing with the eyes is a distinctly feminine one. Doing this allows you to develop the skill of expressing yourself with only a look, conveying pure meaning to those around you.

Take a pretty scarf and gently hold either end of it in both hands. Raise it up so that all you can see of your face are your eyes and above. First, warm up by slowly looking back and forth, wide and closed, and up and down.

Watching yourself in the mirror, try to smile with only your eyes. Concentrate on your warmth, and the genuine nature coming from within. Try to radiate happiness.

Try other feelings, such as anger, concern, seduction, shyness, or mystery.

Spend a few minutes flirting with yourself in the mirror. Look away, and look back at yourself. Try to add fire to the first moments your gaze connects.

Allow your eyes to dance freely with the music as a way to continue to strengthen them.

Do not over strain your eyes. If yours start to feel tired, stop, and try the exercise again another day.

Make up is another fun way to enhance your eye dancing, but be sure to always wash it off at the end of the day!

What did you think of eye dancing? In what ways can you apply it to your daily life? When do you think this skill might come in handy? What are some other distinctly feminine skills you can think of?

Day Nine:

Make a list of ways you serve other people that you don't do for yourself. Or even things you do for others that you don't expect to get anything back. This can be things like listening to a friend's problems, helping them baby or cat sit, giving advice, or sitting with them in the hospital. Are you always giving rides?

Part of self love and self care is making sure you aren't giving so much that you become depleted. Sadly, "givers" become depleted very quickly in a society full of "takers". It is not selfish to take care of yourself--it is necessary.

For all the ways you consistently do for other people, make an opposite that needs to be met to fulfill *your* needs.

Example: "I am always listening to my old high school friend vent about her job. For every half hour I give her, I will ignore all messages for equal time. I do not have to be available to everyone 24/7."

Day Ten:

Today you can think of your most negative thoughts. We know you and your body are worth love, compassion, and respect...but old habits die hard. Let's try to face old thoughts.

How does your body compare to typical advertisements? What are you "missing" that could make you "ideal" to the media and those around you? Do you agree with these body parameters? Does your race or culture affect your body size? Are you giving yourself impossible comparisons, and unreachable goals?

What do you think is the overall effect of giving yourself goals that you will always fail at?

Let's move on from your body. What do you truly and honestly dislike about yourself? And maybe even...*hate*? What is some way you fall short? Is it possible to fix it? Do you even want to?

We can spend some time wallowing in these thoughts, but after you write your list look at everything there. Imagine this list belonged to anyone else you hold dear. Imagine you had written this list about anyone else! Imagine reading this list to a younger sibling.

It would be a difficult thing to do--coldly and callously reading off cruel judgements and assessments on a person's body, habits, life, learning ability, or spirituality. So why were you able to do it to yourself?

Who taught you to judge yourself so harshly, to not mitigate your own thoughts towards yourself? Who taught you the only person you didn't need a filter for was yourself?

Because sis, let me tell you, you *do* need a filter. The saying goes that you are not the voice in your head--you are the one listening. You don't *have* to listen to untrue bullshit about yourself, least of all from your own brain!

Today, you don't have to do anything, but recognize that it is time for a change. It is time to change the way you talk to yourself. It is time to change the way you incentivize yourself. It's time to respect yourself with the same respect that you give others.

If you have any thoughts, reflect:

Day Eleven:

Try to remember the story of each scar and dimple. Do you remember each mark, or have those memories faded into the corridors of time? Do you have any marks from your childhood abuse? How about any self inflicted?

Do any of your scars or marks (even more innocent ones) cause you shame? Do you try to hide them?

Do you have any beauty marks or birth marks?

Today, try to find and document every mark on your vessel, and simply accept that they are there.

Day Twelve:

Today while in front of the mirror, think about your vulnerabilities. Which do you think of while you sit in this vulnerable state of nakedness? Take the time to really be honest with yourself in this reflection of your lower, or less appealing parts (either to yourself or others).

Questions you can ask yourself include: What are the weakest things about you according to you? What about according to others? Is there anything about your physical appearance you believe makes you vulnerable or weak? What about unattractive? Is there anything you can do to change these things? Is it really the worst thing to have them? What are ways you combat or make up for these these areas in your everyday life?

Day Thirteen:

Yesterday we addressed your weaknesses and vulnerabilities. Today we accept them. Not necessarily as a permanent fixture on our character and personality, but rather as something that has been a part of you (or at least was a burden you chose to carry). For example, someone else may have an opinion of you that you have taken on as your own. Let's go through yesterday's list, and look yourself in the mirror and say out loud you accept it. You can write down your thoughts first, if you enjoy journaling or need to see it written down somewhere.

> For example, "I need to spend time by myself without other people at regular intervals to give myself a break. I accept that. My initial reaction is often overboard. I accept that I do this. My butt is flat. I accept this. My hair takes longer to take care of than other people. I accept this. I cannot change my childhood. I accept this. I will never have a parent or guardian who truly cared about me in my childhood. I accept this."

Day Fourteen:

Have you ever wondered what it is like to be an artist's muse? To languish in front of someone and have their eyes devour your skin, inspired by every glorious inch?

Well, let's be our own muse. Today we are going to do a set of quick self-sketches. Use a pencil or colored pencils, follow the prompts, and have fun! This is just another way to observe and enjoy our unique body, as well as a way to stretch the way we see ourselves.

Remember, the only rule is to be totally inspired by the gorgeous person in front of you! Oh yeah, and you know the drill. These are *nudes*!

My face from the forehead up:

Full body portrait:

My left eye:

My butt:

My feet:

My lips:

My breasts:

A side view of my face:

My palms:

My favorite outfit:

My favorite panties:

My favorite body feature:

My least favorite body feature:

A strand of hair from each part of my body:

A Self Portrait From Behind:

Day Fifteen:

Yoni. Pussy. Sacred Space. Vulva. Honey pot. Snatch. Clit.

When you are in front of the mirror today, open your legs and look at yourself...What word are you most comfortable using for your genitalia? Do you prefer it when people use forward terms, or do you prefer slang and nicknames? I know it's probably more correct to say vagina, but in the moment of conversation, I usually call it a "cooter"--as in "I love my cooter!"

Right now, find the term you feel most comfortable using for your own body...There are hundreds in common use, but you can also make a personal name. Perhaps choose one that means something powerful, or kind, but most of all empowering.

Do you feel empowered now, looking between your legs? Why or why not? What power do you feel this few inches of your body has? What power does it lack? Do you think it is beautiful? Why do you think this? Would you change what you have or how it looks if you could?

Day Sixteen:

Let's continue looking at your sacred space today. Regardless of whether or not you believe your genitalia is attractive or not, set a timer and spend 10 minutes just looking at your own body. While you look, meditate on how special and unique you are. How wonderful it is you have these particular features.

Remember that no one else in the world looks exactly like this, and it is a wonderful gift for yourself and others. Understand your body is normal and beautiful, no matter what advertisements and social media portray or uplift. Remember your genitals are worth love and pleasure, just as all people. There is nothing wrong with your genitals or how they look.

Write about how you feel about your genitals after the exercise.

Day Seventeen:

Yesterday you stared at your sacred space. Today, draw it. Sketch it out as best you can, adding color if you would like. Draw as though you are portraying someone you love very much. Draw it several times and at

different angles if you would like. Be as abstract or detailed as you want--
there is no wrong interpretation of your own vagina!

Day Eighteen:

By now you are like Tahtahme, I get it, it's a pretty pussy, can we put it
away? No. We have one more exercise, and this is one I hope you will
continue to use as a weekly ritual for the rest of your life.

Find a place either in your home where the sun shines in nice through the window, or a place outside you can be private. If outside I would suggest wearing a dress and no panties if you are worried about being seen.

Lay down and open your legs and let the sun and air touch your portal. Rest like this for a few minutes (only! Especially at first!), and really feel this caress. Perhaps play one song that you feel will fit the mood or help you relax.

This ritual an opening and surrendering act. In as many ways submissive as it is liberating. You are exposed and empowered, yet in a vulnerable position.

Write about how this made you feel both physically and spiritually.

Day Nineteen:

List 10 important attributes or characteristics you inherited directly from your parents, guardians, or heaviest influence growing up. Why was this an important thing to learn? Did they teach you this on purpose? Through actions or through words?

Example of attributes: My mother taught me how to be a giving person...My uncle gave me my zeal for life and adventure.

Day Twenty:

Optimal womb health, including spiritual and physical cleansing, cannot be fully achieved unless your body is able to detox from the toxins it is holding.

This means it is time to make a change in your diet. Your womb holds on to everything--both the negative and the positive.

To detox the womb, meat and dairy need to be cut out of the diet. The colon can begin to grow heavy due to meat and dairy, which both can take hours, days, and even weeks and months longer than plant foods to go through the system.

Directly under the colon is, you might have guessed, your womb! To relieve this weighty pressure from your womb, you need to give your body fibrous foods that will cleanse you from the inside.

Colon Healthy Foods:

- Celery
- Broccoli
- Whole Grains
- Pears
- Oranges
- Alfalfa
- Spirulina

Womb Healthy Foods:

- Berries
- Legumes
- Cabbage
- Sprouted Seeds
- Green Tea
- Nettle Tea

Today, eat one food that is healthy for the womb, and write down some ways you can change your diet to be a more womb-healthful one.

Day Twenty One:

Castor Oil Pack

A castor oil pack is a traditional womb healing method of soaking a cloth in castor oil, and applying it to the womb area. The castor oil soaks out toxins, promoting both cleansing as well as blood circulation. Castor oil packs also stimulate the lymphatic system, and liver function.

Use of a castor oil pack is both spiritual and physical. If you are having cramps, a castor oil pack can help remove the symptoms. Similarly, if your womb feels empty or void, or has suffered recent trauma, a castor oil pack can help cleanse and relieve symptoms as well.

The womb is around 4 finger widths below your navel. When using a castor oil pack, be sure to wear clothes that you do not mind getting dirty. Leave the pack on for 45-80 minutes, keeping your body relaxed and rested.

After you remove the pack, feel free to give yourself a gentle massage. Do not try to move your womb around, rather take this moment as an opportunity to connect with your womb, see how she is doing, and come to know her better than you have before. Even though you are gentle, do not be afraid to add pressure. Do your best to keep the experience feeling good and positive. If you feel you need to take this further, consider hiring a traditional womb massager to spend time checking and aligning your womb.

There is a power to touching your own womb, and using your own hands to heal. Beyond that, it is an intimate process, coming to know your womb from the outside in this way. Especially during times of womb pain, overcome shyness and get to know your body, and listen to what your womb is saying that it needs.

Reflection and Notes:

Day Twenty Two:

Write small, positive prayers on plain notecards (or type and glue, but you want the cards to be sturdy!). This is a beautiful moment to be simply grateful, ask for safety and protection, and ask for whatever it is you may need. Decorate your cards and place in an organza drawstring party bag with dried herbs (suggestions listed below).

Find somewhere accessible to put it, such as your purse, car, night table, or backpack. Place somewhere you will remember it or see it often-- do *not* put it in your purse if your purse is a black hole where things disappear for months! Use a sturdier drawstring bag and tie it to the outside if you need to and don't hesitate to be creative to make things meet your needs.

Prayer Suggestions:

- Nothing is going to happen today that I cannot handle.

- May no one undo me, drain me, or bring calamity to my doorstep.

- Above all else, guard your heart, for everything you do flows from it. • Proverbs 4:23

- Let the wind push me in the right direction as I journey down this path.

- I am art. I am authentic. I am love. I am me. • Malebo Sephodi

- The moments of our life are not expendable, And the possible circumstances of death are beyond imagination. If you do not achieve an undaunted confident security now, What point is there in your being alive, O living creature? • Padmasambhava, The Tibetan Book of the Dead

- Get wisdom. Though it cost all you have, get understanding • Proverbs 4:7

- It is not too late to accomplish the greatness that rests eagerly in my soul.

- Ancestor's guide me and give me strength.

- I want to take a minute, and remember to say, "Thank you. I am grateful for all that I have and all that I am."

- A heart at peace gives life to the body • Proverbs 14:30

- I rise like the sun above olive trees, like the moon above date palms. Where there is light, I shall be. Where there is darkness, there is none of me. I am counted as one among stars. • Book of Coming Forth By Day

Herb Suggestions (for the bag):

- Rosemary

- Basil

- Oregano

- Lavender

- White Sage

- Eucalyptus

- Clove

- Ylang Ylang

- Sandalwood

- Bay Leaves (place in the bag whole, when done praying, write a wish, small prayer, or heart's desire and burn the leaf)

Write a genuine prayer from your heart, asking for those things you truly desire to gain from healing from your childhood sexual abuse.

Which prayers did you include? Which herbs? Why?

Day Twenty Three:

Finish these haikus while sitting in front of the mirror naked. Remember, a haiku is a traditional Japanese poem that is three lines long, with the first and the last being 5 syllables, and the second being 7. I have written the first line of a few here for you to begin getting the ideas flowing. Draw an image, symbol, doodle, or self portrait on the side to accompany the words.

1)

In the depths I wait.

_____

_____

2)

_____

_____

Self indulgent love.

3)

_____

Revenge too small for the crime

_____

4)

The truth of it is,

_____

_____

5)

_____

_____

_____

6)

_____

_____

_____

7)

_____

_____

_____

8)

_____

_____

_____

9)

_____

_____

_____

10)

_____

_____

_____

Day Twenty Four:

Goddess Bath

A Goddess Bath is an excellent tool for spiritual cleansing, to come back into your center of peace and positivity, to wash away negative thoughts, to gaining new ideas, to think something over, to clear your mind, and to talk to your ancestors.

More commonly called a "spiritual" or "sacred" bath, this is a way of spending time with and on yourself. My suggestion is to bath between the hours of 4-6am for maximum clarity and openness to the spirit. Much of the healing comes from the very act of taking the time in your day to relax in the tub.

Another importance of bathing over showering is having the water welcome your entire body in. Water does not discriminate against any body type or body part. It touches and heals all equally. If you do not have a bath, then a shower is of course fine...it is always best to just use what you have and not sweat the details. Remember to focus on your desires.

Tools Needed:

- A bathtub
- 2 pitchers or bowls

- 1 lemon (pulls harmful toxins from the skin, detoxes, refreshes)

- 1/2 Tsp cayenne pepper (can substitute with anything fine powdered and hot, used for cleansing as well as adding a "kick" or quickness to your goal of peace)

- 1/2 Tsp Cinnamon (soothes, relaxes, invigorates, heals)

- 1/2 Tsp Grapefruit Essential Oil (antidepressant, joyous)

- Drop of your favorite Oudh oil or other oil fragrance.

- Dried or fresh rose petals (self love, femininity).

- Other dried flowers that you feel resonate with your inner femininity.

- Candles to decorate the bathroom

- A beautiful, feminine playlist that can be played uninterrupted by advertisements.

- Simple, loose dress in white (or preferred color).

1) Fill your bathtub with comfortably warm water. Add the rose petals and dry flowers. Light candles and incense around the room (remaining safe). Turn on your music.

2) In the first pitcher or bowl, squeeze the juice of one lemon and put the cayenne pepper. Fill with cold water.

3) In the second pitcher, add the cinnamon, vanilla, and personal fragrance. Fill it with hot water.

4) Place both pitchers where they can be easily accessed during the bath.

5) Enter the tub. Allow your body to relax in full. Concentrate on the deliciousness of your nakedness and vitality. Think about the power in your womanhood as well as the weaknesses. Consider how it is give and take, how to have one, you must have the other.

6) When you are ready, pick up the pitcher or bowl with the cold water and cayenne pepper. Hold it up as if an offering.

7) Say, "I banish that which holds me back. I release that which I never needed to carry. I cleanse myself with these waters. I release the

grief and pain I have carried in my life, and accept my new path with open arms. I am surrounded by my ancestors, and I face my destiny with poise and strength. Ase."

8) Pour the water on the top of your head steadily and smoothly, feeling it wash down from the top of your head, down your face and body, and into the tub.

9) Envision your struggles running off of you, anything you feel (either through your own choices or no fault of your own) needs to be released in order for you to move on and grow as an adult who is leaving her past behind.

10)   Relax and place both hands on your womb, feeling the power beneath your palms. Understand your role as not only a woman and a healer of your own body, but as a powerful goddess, brimming with power and possibilities.

11)   Recognize that others constantly place their own limitations on you, and that you will no longer be accepting anyone else's narrative.

12)   Pick up the 2nd pitcher.

13)   Say, "I am a Goddess and a lightbringer. I am a well of peace, gentleness, and strength. I protect what is mine with courage and no hesitation. I carry within my womb great wisdom from all the women who have come before me. I now have the clarity to witness the path of peace in dangerous times, and trust my feet to lead where I will do the greatest good. Ase."

14)   Pour the water, this time leaning your head back so that your face is splashed first, again pouring steadily and smoothly.

15)   Envision every positive attribute you have ever wanted (for example, grace, intuition, fearlessness), splashing in excess all over you, as though from a waterfall or spring shower, puddling around you in it's abundance.

16)   Rise slowly from this well of opportunity around you, and in the same way you Undress With Purpose, now try to dry your body gently and deliberately, not scratching or hurrying across any part.

17)   Put on the dress and spend at least 10 minutes of reflection sitting outside (if the day is nice), or in a comfortable space indoors.

Feel free to expand upon this sacred bathing lesson. Experiment with various herbs, salts, and scents and make the Goddess Bath truly your own!

Reflect:

Day Twenty Five:

Self Touch Ceremony

Begin by setting the mood for yourself. Groom yourself accordingly, put on the lotions, makeup, and perfumes that you prefer. Undress slowly while you watch yourself. Light candles and incense. Spread flowers around the room. Put on music that makes your heart expand and your soul wander.

Be sure the place you will be sitting or lying is soft and secure. Get yourself comfortable (if you can, in front of a mirror).

Before you touch yourself, remember that your body deserves pleasure, and deserves positive attention. Marvel at the beauty it is already displaying as it waits for your touch.

Using a massaging oil (or almond oil, coconut, etc.), begin the ceremony with a slow application on your whole body of the oil.

Start with lightly massaging your face, gently dragging the fingers upward. Your face has so much character, so much life. It is a divine incarnation of those who came before you, a pleasant mix of 1 million destinies surrendered to one point.

Next the neck, using the pads of your fingers to check for any tender points of soreness. Treat it tenderly for the service it provides your head and thoughts, each inch of skin glorious in its purpose.

Try to take your time even as you massage your shoulders and arms, each hand and finger, your breasts. Oil each nipple, each crease, any stretch marks or folds.

Appreciate the depths of yourself, the wisdom of your body as it reacted and adapted to each turn your life has taken. It carried you. It witnessed with you. It was there with you.

Skip over your yoni for now and massage each thigh all the way around, use the pads of your fingers to caress each dimple of cellulite, each hair growing wild, each birth mark, each inch.

Lay on your stomach and feel every inch of your butt cheeks, massage oil into any rough or sore patches. Jiggle it around, allow it to relax. Spend a second and just relax until you are ready to sit back up again.

Continue massaging oil down your legs, care for your calves, nourish your ankles, rub each foot. Take tender care of the soles of your feet.

When you are finished, wash your hands. Come back to your comfortable space and relax for a moment. Oil your hands again, (and keep handy one of the Do It Yourself lubricant suggestions below).

Focus on your breathing, steady, full, deep, slow. In, out. Look yourself in the eyes. Smile at yourself. Be genuine. You are happy to be here with yourself, happy to be taking this journey.

Begin massaging the outside of your vagina. Do not touch the inside yet, not even the Labia Minora, but do not try to avoid giving your body pleasure from the outside only.

Run your hands around the crease of your thigh, around the outer labia, and up to the womb. Use the warmth to comfort your body.

Whether in a mirror or not, look at your body as you massage it. Watch how it responds to the rubbing of these muscles. Look at how beautiful your moisturized skin is, how it responds so well to the special treatment of an often neglected area.

Once your body has relaxed, gradually work your way to the inner lips.

Do not rush, but continue to explore your body bit by bit. Use your fingers to press and reassure each inch of skin, keeping your breathing steady. You have plenty of time and can be as gentle as you want.

Slowly work your way inside of your body, using as many fingers as you are comfortable with. Still focus on massage, even then. Apply various amounts of pressure--keep in mind there is no rush. See if you are tense anywhere on the inside. Try to really explore your body in a way you haven't before. For the sake of exploration as well as healing.

If you have never touched your own cervix, today could be an excellent first time. Continue to reach your fingers back until you feel a small bump in the back. Nothing can get lost in this small chamber--it is a small space, but such a powerful and intriguing one.

Do not be shy about wanting or needing to insert more fingers, or to add more lubricant--this is your pleasure time! A soft, inviting vagina is one that is turned on and happy. Enjoy the experience of simply spending time with yourself, enjoying your own body.

This small space is yours to cherish and enjoy. Finish this ceremony in whatever way you need to be satisfied. Experiment and try new massage oils, positions, and types of touch--there is no wrong answer to self pleasure. Spending time learning what your body enjoys is a beautiful way to continue to connect with yourself and know yourself on deeper levels.

As you grow on your self love journey, self touch will evolve more positively every time. Do not be afraid to repeat the ceremony often, allowing your words and movements to change as you get to know your personal taste better, and really come to relish the time spent on yourself.

DIY Self Touch Lubricants:

- Sweet Snatch Oil: 1 cup coconut oil, 1tbsp high quality honey, 2 drops ylang ylang essential oil.

- Tingle Rub: 1 cup coconut oil, 2 drops peppermint essential oil, 1 drop black pepper essential oil.

- Calming Wetness: ¼ cup flax seed oil, ¼ cup aloe vera gel, 2 drops lavender essential oil, 1 drop jasmine essential oil.

How did it feel to spend that kind of time on yourself? Have you ever given yourself a full body massage before? Have you ever touched the inside of your vagina before? What do you think about touching yourself inside? How does it feel? Did you learn anything new about yourself through this exercise (spiritually, mentally, physically)?

Day Twenty Six:

Today can we try to forgive ourselves? Maybe you really made a huge mistake and it altered your whole life. Maybe it wasn't totally your fault, but you still kinda hate yourself for it.

Whatever it is, you cannot change it now. And you have already tried not forgiven yourself. You've been walking around with a bone to pick with yourself for years.

When you can't forgive someone, your anger seeps throughout your body like poison, weakening you as time goes on. When you can't forgive yourself, the poison works much more quickly.

Write down the any things, big or small, that you kind of blame yourself for, or are angry with yourself for acting or reacting the way you did. Maybe it's a time you replay in your head often, where you wish with every fiber you had done the whole thing differently. Maybe you think if you hadn't been so *you* the situation would have changed.

Whatever it is, write it down. Read it out loud. Savor it. Consider if your long bout of punishing yourself, really fit the crime. Were you even guilty? Can you forgive yourself, and never know to never forget the lesson?

It may take a few tries, but slowly release the burden. Again, not the lesson. Just the burden. Just the hatred. Just the pain. Say, "I forgive myself."

If you hurt someone else, write them an apology. Tell them you are sorry, and why. Let them know the impact the moment had and how you are forever changed because of it. If need be, ask for their forgiveness too.

If you want to, or even can, you may send your letter. But this isn't necessary. You do not need to invite your whole past back in. Forgiving yourself, was the true point of this exercise, apologizing to someone else in person or in spirit, is simply a way to bring the exercise full circle, depending on your situation.

Day Twenty Seven:

Anywhere in the world there are women, there is dancing. Even the most sexually repressed societies know of wild women who gyrate by the light of the moon--and fear them.

But why? What is this power a woman wields that everyone is so afraid of?

The Divine Feminine.

Femininity is squashed down it seems everywhere we turn. And when it's not being squashed out, many of us are throwing it to the wayside in an effort to not be saddled by its burdens.

Now am I saying femininity is the only way to break your way out in this world, sis? No. But I am going to let you in on the secret that typically elder women pass down when able: Being able to wield your femininity is a powerful, powerful tool to have.

Just like eye dancing allows you to cultivate the skill of talking with your eyes, feminine dancing in general holds many benefits.

Even if you never seduce another human with your dancing a day in your life, seduce yourself. Dancing gives self confidence and strength. It adds grace--the simple act of using your body helps you gain more control over it.

Size does not matter when dancing with your feminine nature. A woman with no curves and a larger woman can both dance with their feminine nature all the same. A man, for that matter, can dance within his feminine nature, and I am sure you have seen men who you feel can connect with their Divine Feminine better than you can.

Well, it's your birthright to reach out and grab, sis. Let's stop waiting and go ahead and claim it.

Make yourself a music list with songs that make you just want to feel the flow of your body, songs that make you want to move.

Get dressed--or don't! Wrap yourself in a sheer piece of fabric and apply some red lipstick. Where whatever makes you confident. Change clothes several times if you want!

Before you dance, be sure to stretch and do a light warm up so you do not hurt yourself! Keep your dance sessions short in the beginning if you are not used to the exercise.

Try not to confine yourself to certain dances or rules. Combine every feminine dance you know from bellydance to hiproll to hula to twerking to salsa. Give yourself no rule except that your movements should be that of

Divine Feminine Expression. Add in some ballet or modern or jazz. Be sure to give yourself at least a few feet of clear space to express yourself. Be creative with what space you do have.

Do not be scared to try new things--you are the only witness. If you don't pull something off the first time, do not be discouraged! Simply try again or move on for now. As you gain strength, you will also gain skill with practice.

Unleash your inner wild woman. Roll on the floor. Yell. Sing along. Howl. Focus on giving your lungs air, but allow yourself to become tired, your breathe to become ragged. Be free.

Take time to make each body part dance alone. Concentrate on making every movement graceful and precise. Be frugal with your movement--control every muscle.

Be unapologetically yourself. Do not confine yourself to social norms or what you think would necessarily be attractive to others. Be attractive to you. Be confident in that attractiveness. Enjoy the unique properties that create the woman that is *you*.

Song Suggestions:

- In the Morning • Nao

- Fruit • ABRA

- Female Energy • Willow Smith

- Love to Love You Baby • Donna Summer

- Orion • Carolyn Malachi

- Sango • OSHUN

How did it feel to dance today? Do you like dancing? How often do you do it? Do you think you will keep dancing?

Day Twenty Eight:

Make a Bucket List! 50 Things to do before you die, and leave the first 10 spaces for stuff you want to do by this time next year.

1)
2)
3)
4)
5)
6)
7)
8)
9)
10)

11)

12)

13)

14)

15)

16)

17)

18)

19)

20)

21)

22)

23)

24)

25)

26)

27)

28)

29)

30)

31)

32)

33)

34)

35)

36)

37)

38)

39)

40)

41)

42)

43)

44)

45)

46)

47)

48)

49)

50)

Day Twenty Nine:

Read the full list of 100 things you love about yourself to yourself out loud in the mirror. Keep distractions around you minimal. Use a loving, kind, encouraging, and appreciative tone. Say them like you mean it--have no apology behind your tone. Look yourself in the eye as well as all over your body. Look yourself in the eye. Repeat a sentence if you don't believe yourself the first time.

If you haven't finished the list, read what you have so far and keep working on it. If you haven't started it yet, turn to Part 2 and brainstorm 5-10 right now. Read them out loud a few times through.

Reflect:

Day Thirty:

Self Love Healing Spell

Materials:

- ☐ Glass Jar

- ☐ Scissors

- ☐ Flowers gathered from the neighborhood, including roses

- ☐ Pink 7 Day candle (or use what you have)

- ☐ 2 blue candles (optional)

- ☐ Small Mirror

- ☐ 1 Cup Sugar (Brown, Cane, Powdered, or a mix are all fine).

- ☐ Incense

- ☐ Pen

- ☐ Pretty card

- ☐ An Ace of Cups or Hearts from a card deck. Can also use a picture, drawing of yourself, or symbol that represents you.

- ☐ Oil for dressing the candles (can be a bought oil mixture for self love or confidence, or can be as simple as olive oil).

- ☐ Create a personalized mixture of herbs (dried, fresh, or oil extracts are all fine) from the following depending on your needs:

  - Self Love: Jasmine, Allspice, Raspberry, Rose Petals, Vervain, Lavender

  - Strengthen Friendship: Bay, Basil, Eucalyptus, Holly, Catnip, Vanilla, Lemon, Sunflower

  - Raise Self Esteem: White Sandalwood, Chamomile, Licorice Root, Ginseng

  - Self Confidence: Lemon Balm, Valerian, Peppermint, St. John's Wort, Pine

- ☐ Make 8 ounces of a tasty, light, and soothing beverage to meditate over afterwards. Suggestions include:

  - Coconut Milk with Rosewater

  - Lavender Lemonade

  - Chamomile Rose Tea

  - Berry Coconut Smoothie

1) Go on a walk and gather flowers from your neighborhood that catch your fancy. Can include foliage because green is healing, but do need the sweet fragrance and joyful colors of flowers. We gather the flowers instead of buying because we are in a way leaning on and gaining support from the community. If no flowers grow nearby, or you cannot walk in your area, buy a bunch from a local store. Use scissors to make getting them easy as well as less harmful to the bushes.

2) Sit nude or in beautiful, comfortable clothes. You can be in front of a large mirror or outside with nature.

3) Gently pull the petals off of the flowers and place in the glass jar. Think about each of the small attributes that come together to create a whole person. Consider the beauty and effort of each petal, and how each had to struggle to grow the same as their neighbor. Note imperfections and how the flower is still a beautiful flower despite these.
Small flowers and buds can be placed in whole for beautiful effect.

4) In the card, write all of the qualities you have already that you admire about yourself. Then write all of the wonderful qualities that you are capable of and are cultivating for your future. Take your time and put care into your penmanship. Decorate the page if it is plain paper.

5) Place the card/letter in the jar (folding if you must).

6) Pour in as much sugar as you feel you need to sweeten your attitude towards yourself.

7) Place the Ace of Cups/Hearts (or picture) in the center of the mirror, and put the jar on top of the card.

8) Put the pink 7 Day Candle directly behind the jar, off of the mirror.

9) Dress the two blue candles with oil, rubbing from top to bottom, and feeling the warmth of self satisfaction and contentment.

10) Use your herb mixture and sprinkle a circle of the herbs around each candle and the jar as well.

11) Light the pink candle. Close your eyes and really *feel* the woman that you want to be. Imagine what she looks like, how she sounds. Imagine yourself in a state of total contentment with who you are and what you have become. Imagine that you have made the solid choices to become who you have always dreamed of being.

12) Light the blue candle on the bottom left. Say, "I rise with the confidence of my most powerful ancestors. I harness the boldness of the women who came before me, and step forward unafraid and

unapologetic of who I am. I am a woman of great gifts and poise, and there is nothing I cannot accomplish."

13) Light the final blue candle. Say, "As I light this candle, I illuminate within myself a new path of fortune and greatness. I watch as daily these qualities come into me, and become me. I grant myself passage through new spiritual paths and settle back to enjoy the woman I have become."

14) The ancient Egyptian word for magic was *hekau* (pronounced heck-ah-ooo), which translates to literally mean "words of power". To offer power to this spell, take this moment before the lit candles to chant or sing *hekau* until you feel it is time to stop.

15) When you are finished and ready to leave the candles to burn, light incense as your final act. Place it so the smoke floats near the jar.

16) Sit and drink the entire 8 ounce drink, envisioning that the smoke is self appreciation and love wafting into your life, room, and mind. Allow the candles to burn until the 7 Day Candle has burned completely (usually within 4-5 days of lighting).

17) When you clean up the pieces to your spell, save the jar on an altar (either a personal one, or an ancestor altar if you would like to ask for extra help). Do not open the jar until at least one year has passed before checking to see which qualities you gained in the past year (it may help to write a date on a sticky note and put it on the bottom of the jar).

If you feel the need to repeat the spell before the year is finished, do not open your old jar, simply make a new one. Be patient with yourself-- change rarely happens overnight!

Reflect:

Pendulum Reading

A tool that served as my first form of "divination" and a huge help for my growth in self knowledge and healing was learning to read a pendulum.

A pendulum is a weight suspended from a string or chain so that it can swing freely. It can be used to read energy and answer a question with your own intuition. A pendulum is only a tool to aid with ease and clarity of the answers--it is useful especially for when you can't quiet your mind, make a decision, need to follow your heart, or are trying to be clear and concise. It is great for people who need visuals as well.

Either purchase a pendulum or make one by putting something heavy on the end of a string, or simply use a necklace with a weighted charm on the end. The string or chain should be around 6" long, and does *not* need to be longer. Hold the pendulum comfortably in your fingers.

Establish the answer "yes" by asking the pendulum to rotate in a clockwise direction. Do *not* move your hand; use only the energy from your thoughts. Ask it to stop, or show you "void" and wait for it to still. Establish "no" by having it rotate in a circle counterclockwise, opposite of yes. Have the pendulum stop. Last, establish "neutral" by having the pendulum sway back and forth from you, or to and away.

The pendulum can be a powerful tool of self divination and discernment. It can challenge your perceptions of your health and wellness, and serve as a neutral guide to your own inner intuition. Try not to ask the pendulum in a state of anguish and high emotion, but rather in a wiser place of seeking the honest truth for the overall betterment of self. It is not a tool for divining the future, but rather for divining yourself.

Example Questions for Your Pendulum:

Am I afraid of my feelings?

Will I know myself better after doing this exercise?

What age am I emotionally halted at? (Count rotations)

Am I angry (sad, disappointed) in _____?

Does she blame me for what happened?

Is this a healthy food for my body/womb at this time? (hold pendulum over food)

Will doing _____ benefit my womb?

Should I do this cleansing bath/ritual tonight?

Is my stress over this causing my headaches?

Hold the pendulum over your womb, heart, and mind to read a positive, negative, void, or neutral reading. Note how fast or slow the pendulum moves, or how many times it spins.

Reflect:

[Part Three]

Facing What Happened

(A Mourning Period)

It can be extremely difficult to think in detail about the betrayal that you experienced from someone else in your community who you should have been able to trust. I understand that this section could be difficult for you. It was so, so hard for me. It took me years, *years* to face what happened. I am both prideful and stubborn. My ego, probably much like yours absolutely *loathed* this experience.

I am a writer, and it literally poisoned my soul that this chapter was written upon my book, and worst of all when I was least able to defend my blank pages. A child.

I was sad. Broken. I had not yet mourned that child. Mourned a child who sobbed, but was not held. Mourned a child who only wanted to be wanted. Mourned a child who thought she had a safe world. Mourned a child who only wanted some adult who loved her enough to protect her. Mourned a child who prayed this was normal because she didn't like it. Mourned a child who was scared *she* was caught when she suspected people knew.

Mourned a child who needed a world where she was valued, appearance, emotion, and all. Mourned a child whose prayers went unanswered. Mourned a child who dreamed of a savior that never came. Mourned a child who kinda had to save herself.

All this grief inside me that I had carried for years. It was literally heavy on my heart. I carried it on my shoulders at every given moment, remembering at the most inconvenient times. It was like I was haunted by every negative emotion I could muster in a seemingly never ending cycle. Whenever I would think I was "over it"...I wasn't even close.

While I worked through my journey, I found one of the more releasing experiences was facing what happened exactly. And not only facing what happened, but working through every thought I really had in relation to my abuse as a child, and sexual abuse against children in general.

This exercise isn't technically about having a witness...I do firmly believe that you should keep whatever elements of your story you think should never be shared or see the light of day to yourself. There are moments of my abuse that will never see the light of day again--the one time they happened in real life was already too much, and I will not invite them back.

Here we will only write down the thoughts. Facts. What happened. How you saw it then. How you see it now. What you really think. Every gory detail. All of it.

Skip questions that don't apply to you or you don't feel like answering, but try your best to be honest. We aren't sending anyone to jail, or publishing a tell-all autobiography. We are simultaneously donning the hat of the warrior who fought in the battle and the historian desperate to write down the tale.

Give immense interest to the details of your own story. Ponder every angle. Break down those hours, days, moments.

This is your story. Someone else wrote some bullshit into your chapters, well this is the part where we take a pen to the margins and write our own thoughts in. Yes sis, this is *your* story. And when we face it, we own it.

What was the first time you remember someone touching you sexually as a child?

Write in detail about the abuser in this situation. Who were they? How old were they? Why were they trusted alone with you? How did your relationship affect how you felt about what they did to you?

Were they your only abuser? Talk about any others here.

Why do you think your abuser(s) chose you?

How much of your childhood would you say was spent being abused in some way?

Were you sexually abused before you can remember? Write about what you have heard happened. Do you believe it? Why?

Do people believe you now when you tell them of your abuse?

Have you ever been let down by someone's reaction to hearing your abuse? What happened?

Is there a reason it is hard for others to believe you? For example, was your abuser another child? A family member more beloved than you? Did you not react in a way that others would have, which causes people to question your honesty? Do you think that their judgment of the situation is fair or accurate?

Were you able to tell someone about the abuse right away? Were you able to tell someone who could help you? Why did you trust this person?

If you had no one to tell, or no one you trusted enough to tell, why was that?

Did you end up telling much later about your about your abuse? Why do you think you waited? How did it go? Do you think it would have gone better if you told sooner?

Did you ever end up getting the police involved? What did they do? Was that the right choice for you?

Did your abuser ever serve time in jail or prison for their pedophilic abuse? How do you feel about that?

Who do you blame directly for your abuse as a child. Name names and point fingers.

Where was God when you were being abused as a child? Where were your ancestors? Where were the angels, benevolent spirits, saints, and Goddesses?

Have you been sexually abused since childhood ended?

Do you think you will ever be sexually abused again?

If someone tried to sexually abuse you sometime today, how do you *wish* you could respond?

If someone tried to sexually abuse you today, what do you think is the *best* response you could have? Why?

If someone tried to sexually abuse you today, how would you *honestly* react?

If you have a child (or want one), what are ways you would prevent what happened to you from happening to them?

What are ways you think our society fails to stop the sexual abuse of children? What are ways our society condones the sexual abuse of children?

Why do you specifically think it's wrong to be sexually intimate with a child? What does a child lose when they are sexually abused? Does a child gain anything from sexual abuse?

Have *you* ever abused someone (in any way, sexually, physically, mentally, emotionally.... when you were a child *or* as an adult)? What happened? Why did you do it? Have you done it since this time?

Would you consider yourself an abuser? Have you apologized to the person you abused? What is a way you could try to make things better or right with them? Do you think you will ever abuse someone again?

Are you capable of sexually abusing a child today? Do you think you ever will be?

What are ways you personally try to stop the sexual abuse of children?

Are there laws that you think are unfair for stopping people aged 18+ from having sexual relationships with people under the age of 18?

Do you think the law gives fair punishment to people who sexually abuse children? What do you think is adequate punishment for this type of abuser?

How do you think the abuse you endured as a child has affected your sex life today?

Have any of your partners (romantic or sexual) ever pointed out behaviors that you attribute to your childhood sexual abuse? What behaviors? Was it something you could change?

Do you ever find yourself thinking of child sexual abuse at inappropriate or inconvenient times? When? What thoughts? What do you do?

Do you think the abuse affected your sexuality?

Do you think your abuse shaped your views towards sex?

Do you think the abuse affected your views towards gender (in general, or a specific gender)?

Do you think the abuse affected your views and feelings towards marriage?

Do you think your abuse affected your general views and feelings towards most types of relationships?

Do you think the abuse made you more uninhibited or reserved about sex and sexual acts as an adult? Is this a good or bad thing?

What are ways you avoid thinking about your abuse or abuse in general during your daily life? Do you think it is okay to have these thoughts? Why or why not?

Give me 5-10 *benefits* of you having occasional thoughts about childhood sexual abuse:

Do you think a pedophile could be rehabilitated? Why or why not?

Should all pedophiles go to jail?

Do you think people are right who judge pedophiles? What about judging people who are attracted to children, but never act on it?

How many times have you been to therapy over this? Has it worked? What has worked best for you? Is there a way to recreate that in your home?

When did you start to notice you were adversely affected (in any way) by the sexual abuse in your childhood?

What made you decide to heal from this trauma?

Create a superhero whose sole purpose in life is to save childhood sexual abuse victims. What is their gender? Age? Backstory? Include a drawing.

Create an Archangel of Revenge for Sexually Abused Children. Give them a story and picture.

Write in morbid detail a fictional tale where your abuser gets what they deserve:

[Chapter Four]

Letting It Go

It may seem like a tremendous thing after writing down every last meticulous detail. Why live through it again just to let it go?

This is the ultimate release of that which clearly isn't serving you. I am not talking about your opinions or memories. I am talking about the severe, crippling emotional attachment. Your inability to move on and allow yourself to be at peace with where you are and the unique way you view the world. We need you to the point where you understand that what you offer the world at this moment in time is precious and irreplaceable, exactly because of your experiences and how you personally reacted to them.

We have been looking your past in the eyes. Listening to it explain itself. And now we are saying, "Goodbye." And that's *huge* when you really think about it.

This chapter is a compilation of ways to say
that goodbye. Goodbye to the anger, fear and hurt. Goodbye to your abuser's control over you. Goodbye to living in the past.

We aren't *forgetting* anything. But we *are* letting go of the power it has over us.

Only continue if you are truly ready. It is okay if you aren't. You can always come back when you are.

If you are ready, though, might I say it? Welcome back, sis. Welcome back. You are at the doorway to it all. Sanity. Weightlessness. Happiness. Step through the door and leave the baggage you were given behind. It isn't yours and doesn't own you, and you do *not* have to carry it anymore.

Welcome back.

What are 7 *positive* parts of your life today that you know 100% wouldn't have happened if you had not been abused?

What skills do you now have because you were sexually abused as a child?

What are services and work you can perform for other people because you were sexually abused?

What is advice you can offer other adult survivors of childhood sexual abuse?

When was a time you were able to connect with and uplift someone else, because you were sexually abused?

What are signs you now know to look for to spot a sexually abused child?

What are signs you now know to look for to recognize a pedophile and/or an adult manipulating a child sexually?

What are 10 things you have learned on your journey to heal yourself, that you would have never known otherwise?

What are things about you that changed that you *like* about yourself that wouldn't have changed if you weren't sexually abused?

What are some valuable lessons you embodied because of the sexual abuse you endured as a child?

Draw your Goddess self, walking the path of a goddess--a path of self love and self care. Look at yourself with a loving eye.

Write Them A Letter

Is there anything you wish you could tell your abuser(s)? Write a letter here, no holds barred. Don't censor yourself, let them know just how fucked up they are. How much they betrayed you. What they took. Maybe your relationship with them was more complex. Explain how that affected the situation as well.

I don't recommend sending this or any letters. It is my humble opinion that our abusers do not deserve to look on us again, do not deserve to get an ounce of our energy. But I am not you. Do whatever you must for your own unique situation.

My suggestion is to take the letter from the next page, and a candle (or just some matches) and go outside alone somewhere in nature.

Read your letter passionately out loud. Use gestures. Scream. Get rude and personal. Rage. Be sincere.

Burn it.

Dear _____,

You know what this is about.

Reflect:

Get a Witness

Have you ever had a conversation with someone about your sexual abuse? I am talking about with someone who is 100% unapologetically on your side, someone who wishes they could go back in time dual wielding berettas and save your childhood type.

If you have a partner, trusted friend, or loving relative to rely on, it may be incredibly releasing to speak through the pain and allow the words to wash away...be sure to let the person know what you expect--for example, do you want them to remain silent? To never ask questions? Are they allowed to interrupt? Are they allowed to touch or hold you at any point in the process? Let them know your needs so that the experience is successful.

You can repeat this exercise, but only with one person at a time. This avoids overwhelming emotions and better gauge of both participants well being.

Find a private place where you two can hear each other. Try to be comfortable, but not crowded. I would personally suggest somewhere in one of your homes, where you can make tea and a cookie and fruit tray to indulge in during or afterward.

Bring along your workbook (or whatever you have been writing in) and read out loud. Let the wind carry each word away as you release your story into the open, right to a receptive audience and beyond that, into the world.

If you find yourself crying, that is fine. If you know you can continue, keep going! If you don't know if you can, go until you can't any more. Do your best.

If your witness is upset about the crying, let them know that you need this. You need a witness. You need to make it through this. Ask them to hear you out.

When you are finished, don't forget to thank your witness. And don't forget to thank yourself for making it this far.

Reflect:

Put Them In A Jar

If you have already forgiven/ let go of what your abuser did to you, or if you believe in passive karma and letting bygones be, this is *not* an activity for you, please keep stepping and might I congratulate your immense sense of restraint and dignity, sis, you are one of the pure ones, and there ain't many of you left. Might I suggest going and making a flower crown, or getting your nails done while the rest of us do this work?

Is she gone? Good. Let's talk darkness for a second.

So far we have been nice. Real nice. Some might say *too* nice. After all, statistically speaking, your abuser, a pedophile, creep, and overall scumbag, never went to jail for the crime. And while we are at it many pedophiles don't get so much as a stern talking to. And even if they *did* go to jail, can anything really *repay* what they took? Can this person really be trusted to run wild in society after what they did to you?

So maybe you still got a little kick and a few jabs in you? Maybe you think *something* must be done and *someone* has to do it. Fair enough, sis, fair enough.

I got you.

But you need to promise me this is it. We are going to stop giving that scoundrel your time and energy after this. We are gonna ruin them...and then walk away. No looking back.

May I present "Womb Revenge", a sour jar specifically for getting back at a sexual abuser....

Begin with a clean, empty jar. First, place something of your abuser in the bottom. This can be a picture (mugshots and grainy photos are fine), a business card, their name written on a piece of paper, a trinket of theirs, or even a strand of hair if they are still in your life .

While thinking of your negative feelings towards your abuser, take vinegar and pour it in until the jar is half full.

Most souring jars stop here because that is technically all that you need. But we will keep going because the crime committed against you was so heinous that there is no reason to not go all out. These are all suggestions--choose what you like or what fits with your situation. While you add these ingredients concentrate on what each one is supposed to do...even read it out loud. Desire is where much of the power comes from.

- Add two spoonfuls of hot pepper to quicken the souring of your abuser's life.

- Write on a piece of paper, "I bind _____ from harming any more children." Put the paper in the jar.

- Add razor blades and nails to cause pain in their life.

- Pee in the jar to give yourself dominance over their future.

- Lemon juice for further souring power.

- Small pickles to give impotence...break them or stick needles in them for erectile disfunction.

- Whisky will preserve the spell so it keeps for longer time.

- Ants to slowly eat away at their comfort.

- Spiders for discomfort in their everyday life.

- Broken glass to cut all ties with them.

- Thorns or pins to cause small, continuous pains in life.

- Write anything specific you want to happen and put it into the jar as well.

Sit before the open jar. Look at it. Keep your breath steady. I bet it smells and looks awful. This jar is a literal, physical representation of the pain you carry every day.

You did not start with this. You were innocent and trusting once. Weak, and young, and fending for yourself, at least in the moment that mattered. But you are not so powerless anymore. And you are not so easy to take advantage of. In this moment we will take back the power and give back the pain.

Take both hands and place them on your womb. Breath steadily. Feel the power beneath your fingertips. Feel how your womb has been absorbing it all this entire time, the good all the way to the terrible.

Focus on the negative energy there, built up from years of abuse and pain. It is powerful, but it is destroying you. It should not have been forced within you in the first place.

Say, "I transfer this pain back to the one(s) who gave it to me."

With your hands still flat on your womb, pull them away slowly, envisioning the negative emotions tying you to your abuser being taken out, as though attached to your palms. Put them in the jar and repeat, "I transfer this pain back to the one who gave it to me."

When you are satisfied, close the jar. Give it a good shake.

Place it on a plate away from your usual spiritual work. Put a tealight candle on top and light it.

Every day for the next seven days, shake the jar and light a tealight candle on top, repeating, "I transfer this pain back to the one who gave it to me."

At the end of the 7th day, take the jar outside somewhere private. After shaking one last time, bury it or place it somewhere it won't be seen or bothered.

Leave it and do not look back. That part of your journey is over and does not control you anymore.

Reflect:

"Reclaiming Lolita", A Ceremony

If we have to put a label on this, I would put it in the cleansing category, but to me "Reclaiming Lolita" is closer to a Coming of Age ceremony.

With this simple ceremony, you concentrate wholly on yourself, your own healing and well being, your own past, and of course your own future. You.

You also use this as a chance to apologize to the angry, hurting child within. You are not the one who *should* be apologizing--but how long are you going to wait for the person who stole something so precious from your childhood to apologize? You've already waited so long for an apology that isn't coming, why not give it to yourself?

Begin as we have many times in this book, by Undressing With Purpose. With this ceremony, you can do your hair or nails, or wear jewelry, but keep your body nude.

The ceremony should take place in a private room with enough space for a little movement.

Three candles will be before you on a tray or table, one white representing your past, one pink representing your present, one purple to represent your future. Have three notecards and a pen beside you. Calm music such as neo-soul or chillstep can be playing in the background.

Carve the age(s) you were abused as a child into the white candle (the past).

Carve your name and current age into the pink candle (the present).

On the purple candle, carve attributes you wish to gain and hone by your old age. Examples could be wisdom, courage, or nurturing spirit.

Dress the candles with oil (an oudh or essential oil that aids in positivity works best, but any you have will work) from top to bottom.

On the first notecard, write: "*I love you and release you from your pain. It was not your fault and you deserved better. I am sorry for what happened to you. You are free.*" Place the paper under the white candle, and light it.

On the second card, write, "*My journey is beautiful and all mine. I do not carry burdens with me on my path.*" Place the card under the pink candle, and light it.

On the final card write, *"I am excited for my future. My journey is just beginning. There is still so much to experience and enjoy."* Put this under the purple candle and light it.

Decorate the tray or area around the candles with flower petals, and rejuvenating herbs such as elderberry, cinnamon, mint, rosehips, or passionflower. Light incense and place with the candles.

Turn your music up and get a smudging stick. Light it. Cover each inch of your body with the cleansing smoke. Envision the smoke wisping the pain away, leaving the body renewed.

Begin to dance. At first, try to keep your dancing light and maiden like. Convey innocence. Reclaim the childlike nature that was abused and taken advantage of. Feel the child in your heart. Feel her uninhibited bravery and exuberance towards life. Feel her happiness at getting to just *dance*, and to get to do it in a way she could not before.

Next change your movements to represent the woman. A woman has more responsibilities than a child, but she also partakes in pleasures a child cannot enjoy. A woman can force and also seduce. A woman has power that a child doesn't have--a power over her life and her choices, as well as many of the lives surrounding her. Dance with the knowledge of your power and beauty. Dance with the knowledge of your overflowing potential.

For the final part of your dance, allow yourself to be tired. Sweat. Have a stitch in your side--recognize something might be sore tomorrow. Look your mortality in the face and think of your own ancestors, all around you, supporting you since the beginning. Move with steady purpose, flow with where the music takes you. Be grateful for this opportunity we call life, and humble that you made it this far.

When you finish the dance, sit on the floor and completely relax. End the ceremony with a quiet evening, a Goddess Bath, and time to reflect.

Keep the candles lit until it is time to go to bed.

Reflect:

[Part Five]

The Path of a Goddess

In this final section, I offer tools to remain on the path you have set out upon. These are rituals and methods for staying in your center, for not allowing everything around you to trigger you and undo work you have already completed.

Making an Ancestor Altar

My first suggestion is to dedicate a part of your living space to those who came before you. Even if you do not pray to your.ancestors, this is *very* important.

It does not have to be big or extravagant, but having a place of honor for your ancestors is a beautiful way to remember you are not alone, you do have a purpose, and that you are special wonderfully made. After all, you were once but a dream that someone wished for--an aunt, a grandpa, a parent.

You may come to realize you are comforted by the memories on your altar, that you spend time talking to and remembering those you may have been neglecting.

Your ancestor altar should hold a representation of your ancestors. This could be pictures, ashes, old journals, a lock of hair, a family tree, or a keepsake from the family member. Ancestors can even be famous people from your culture or community, and these can be represented by pictures, literature, sheet music, and more.

Plants can spruce up an altar, as well as crystals and flowers. Candles and incense add beautiful appeal.

Purchase a bottle of one of your ancestor's favorite liquor, and occasionally pour them a shot. Bring them the cigar they used to smoke, or a shell you know they would have enjoyed.

When you pass the altar, say hello. When you are feeling depressed and lonely, pull up a chair and rest. When you pray, sit by your family. You are not alone.

Goddess Baths

My next tip for staying in your center is a reminder to always take a cleansing bath. Self care should become second nature, and these baths (or showers, if that is what you have) are the perfect stress reliever if nothing else.

For more information on Goddess Baths, see Day Twenty Four of the Thirty Day Challenge.

Waistbeads

One of my favorite expressions of femininity is waistbeads. Waistbeads are a traditional practice in many parts of Africa that is done just like it sounds-- tying a string of beads around your waist.

Traditionally worn to show weight gain, tribe, status, fertility, and more, waistbeads are worn by black women in the diaspora as a representation of black pride, the divine feminine, and to track waist size.

Waistbeads can be purchased or made and used to keep track of or celebrate anything you can think of. As a reward for completing this journey, I highly encourage gifting yourself with a new set to grace your hips.

Yoni Eggs

I do not recommend using yoni eggs internally, or really any kind of foreign object penetration while recovering from sexual abuse. Yoni eggs would, however, be a beautiful gift for yourself at the completion of the workbook.

Crystal Yoni eggs can be used externally for healing just like any crystal, and for these reasons I will include reputable, black owned shops to purchase from at the end of this chapter.

Sacred Sunday Sister Circle

The Sacred Sunday Sister Circle is a movement to create an indigenous sisterhood. Open to women of color, you can find it at **patreon.com/sacredsistercircle**. This is a safe place for childhood sex abuse victims, black women, dark skin, and all sexualities. This group is for support through your journey with those on similar paths, or who love supporting others still healing.

Recommended Shops

These stores are ones that I recommend for perusal during your womb healing journey.

- **Sacred Sister Circle**: Every Sunday at 2pmPT, hosted by Tahtahme (the author!) at patreon.com/sacredsistercircle
- **Womb Healing Workbooks**: Search "Tahtahme" at Amazon!
- **The Path of a Goddess**: Womb Healing, Specializing in Postpartum Healing and Sexual Trauma (jujusquare.en/tahtahme)
- **Bohindie** : Waistbeads (www.bohindie.com)
- **Love and Light Healing**: Yoni Steam Kits, Womb Teas, Womb Education (www.loveandlightheal.com)
- **Manifest, The Wholistic Approach**: Yoni Eggs, Womb Wellness Consultations, Massage Therapy and more (www.manifesttwa.com)
- **Oudh of the Royal Bloodline**: Oudh Oils and Other Specialty Products (www.oudhofroyalbloodline.com)

If you think you should be on the recommended shops list in future Womb Healing Workbooks, or if you have any suggestions or comments about the Womb Healing Workbooks, please email Tahtahme at thepathofagoddess@gmail.com

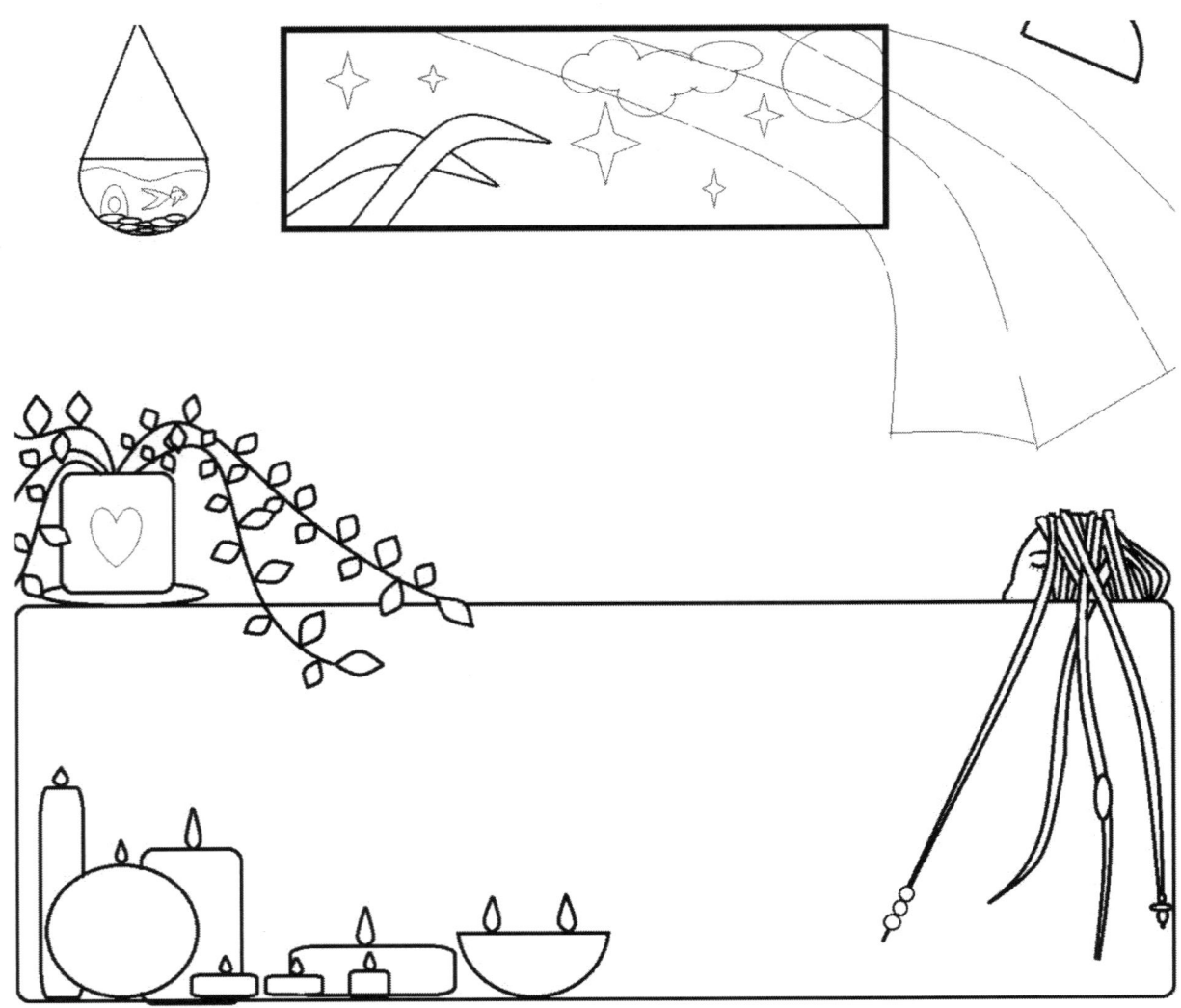

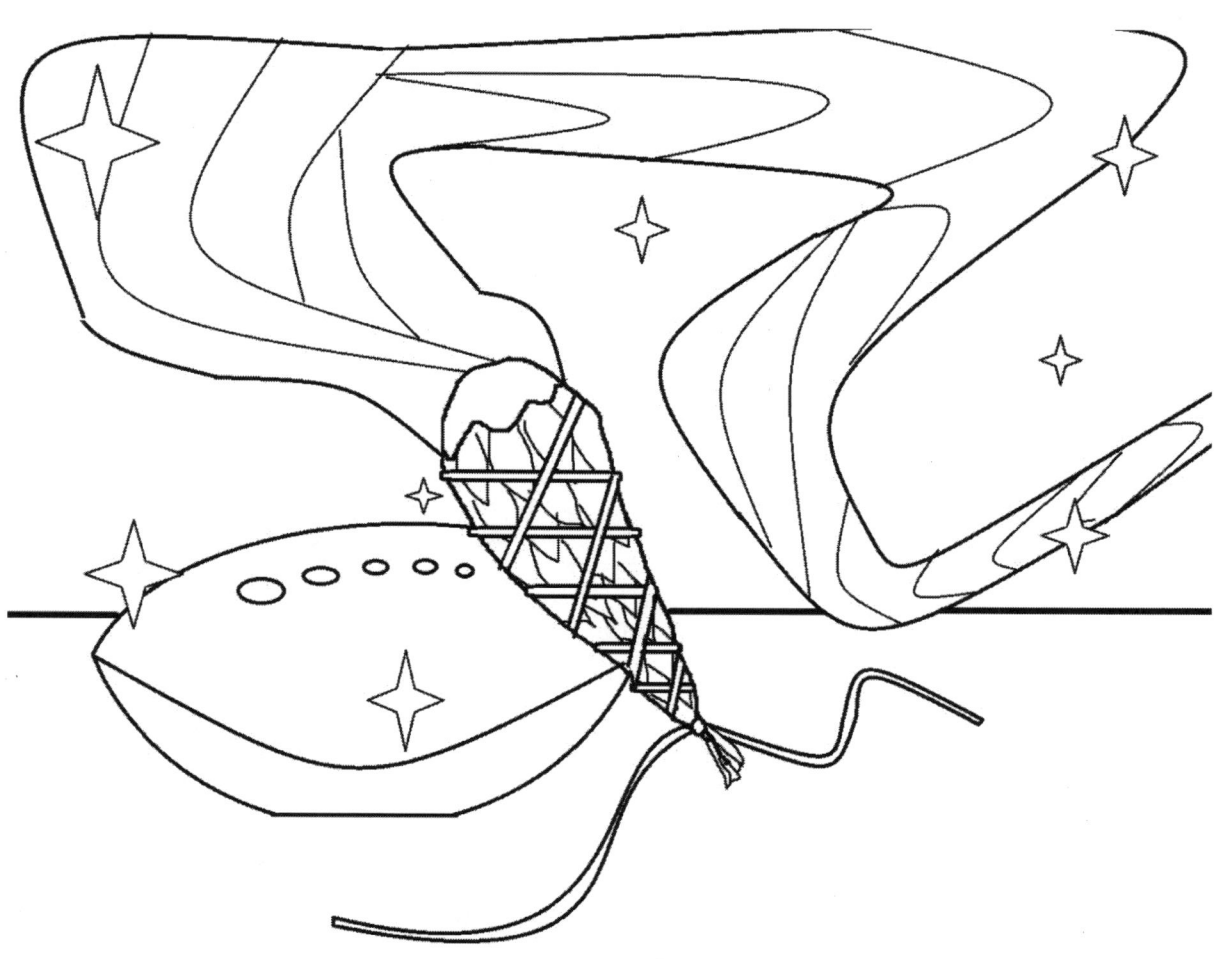

Made in the USA
Coppell, TX
05 May 2022

77366173R00099